CAROL

Kitty IP

HUMBLE TABLE, WISE FARE

1

Living the Dharma

Venerable Master Hsing Yun

©2007 Buddha's Light Publishing
By Venerable Master Hsing Yun
Translated by Tom Manzo, Ph.D. and Shujan Cheng, Ph.D.
Edited by Pey-Rong Lee and Fo Guang Shan International Translation Center
Illustrations by Venerable Won Sung
Book and cover designed by Dung Trieu

Published by Buddha's Light Publishing
3456 S. Glenmark Drive, Hacienda Heights, CA 91745, U.S.A.

ISBN-10: 1-932293-25-6   ISBN-13: 978-1-933293-25-8

Library of Congress Cataloging-in-Publication Data
Xingyun, da shi.
[Selections. English. 2007]
 Humble table, wise fare / by Hsing Yun ; translated by Tom Manzo & Shujan
Cheng.
      p. <1> ; cm.
 Author's selections translated from Chinese.
 ISBN-13: 978-1-932293-25-8 (pbk. : alk. paper)
1. Fo Guang Shan Buddhist Order--Doctrines. 2. Buddhism--Doctrines. I.
Manzo, Tom. II. Cheng, Shujan. III. Title.

 BQ9800.F6392X553213 2007
 294.3'444--dc22

                                        2006100057

Preface

The Vegetable Root Sayings is a Chinese book that was written by Hong Zicheng during the Ming Dynasty. Since then, numerous editions have been printed, with some copies distributed free of charge. Some editions have contained graceful illustrations: a few years ago, the famous Taiwanese cartoonist Tsai Chih Chung produced one such edition, complete with cartoons. I have heard that the book is widely distributed in Mainland China as well. These illustrated editions have increased the circulation of the work. The illustrations not only make it more enjoyable to read but also help people understand the principle of personal conduct. The merits from promoting the distribution of the work are really boundless.

When I was young, I often read *The Vegetable Root Sayings*, familiarizing myself with the content of the book. Later, when I was teaching the Dharma, I was able to quote from it. Over time, I have found that *The Vegetable Root Sayings* is not only brief, to the point, tactful, and charming, but also rich in philosophical and literary elegance; it is popular and yet august. The literary and artistic meaning is so profound and lasting that each saying can serve as a motto for dealing with people and conducting affairs in daily life.

For more than thirty years, everything I have said and done has been for the purpose of teaching the Dharma and educating people's minds. Recently, it occurred to me that some of what I have said is in the same style as *The Vegetable Root Sayings*, and that a collection of these words could be dedicated to the youth of today to serve as a reference for cultivating the body and mind. Joyfully aware of this possibility, some of my Fo Guang Shan disciples began to collect my lectures, diary entries, Dharma talks, and opening speeches-more than 2,000 items in all. For the publication of *Humble*

Table, Wise Fare, I have selected a thousand sayings from among them.

I have four hopes for this publication:

1. The content of this book is a selection of words that I have spoken to people from all walks of life. At this time, our society is promoting spiritual reform. I sincerely hope that by reading this book, people will feel the benefits of purifying the body and mind, and consequently make some contribution to society.

2. I have been busy traveling throughout the world teaching the Dharma. There are always thousands of people who attend these events. However, I regret that I have no way of talking to every individual devotee and friend directly and at leisure. By dedicating this book to them, I hope that it can serve as a bridge to connect our hearts, and thus, to some

degree diminish my regret.

3. In modern education, there is a dearth of books that encourage and promote learning and the cultivation of body and mind. I hope that all students can use this edition as a reference and guidebook for cultivating the mind, and that it will have a profound influence on their future.

4. *Humble Table, Wise Fare*, like the enduring *The Vegetable Root Sayings*, is not delicious gourmet food, but rather the plain vegetables that go with a simple meal. I hope readers can be spiritually invigorated and completely relaxed and happy at this humble table.

Hsing Yun

Acknowledgments

We would like to thank everyone who has supported this project from its conception to its completion: Venerables Hui Chi, Yi Chao, and Miao Hsi for their support and guidance; Tom Manzo and Shujan Cheng for their faithful translation; Pey-Rong Lee for editing the manuscript; Dung Trieu for designing the book; and Kevin Hsyeh for preparing the manuscript for publication. We are especially grateful to Venerable Won Sung for allowing us the use of his beautiful illustrations in our little edition.

The saddest thing in life
Is to have no hope for your own future.
The worst habit in life
Is to have no plan for reaching your goal.

When climbing a cliff,
You need bushes and shrubs most urgently.
When facing life's trials,
You need advice and direction immediately.

The greatest handicap is not a lack of ability,
But a lack of understanding.
The key to success is not your credentials,
But your drive to learn.

By taking the short end of the stick, you can cultivate virtue.

By putting yourself in another's shoes, you can develop compassion.

By accepting things as they are, you can be carefree.

By enjoying without attachment, you can always be happy.

Not harboring anger towards friends brings ease.

Living life without delusion brings happiness.

Having no attachment to perceptions brings forth the pure land.

Cultivating without striving for gain brings nirvana.

Your ability increases when you apply great effort.
Your knowledge grows when you stay humble.

Health is about sound body and mind,
Rather than power and strength.
Longevity is about prolonging wisdom,
Rather than days and years.

In the pursuit of learning, have a joyful attitude.
In offering advice, keep an open mind.
In taking on responsibility, have courage.
In dealing with others, remain respectful.

Everything has its pros and cons,

Simply understand how to weigh them.

Always keep sight of what is possible,

Even dry stones and rotten wood can be used as medicine.

Everyone has strengths and weaknesses,

Simply understand how to bring out the best in others.

Always emphasize the merits of others,

Even broken copper and brittle iron can be forged into steel.

Scorn, bear it.

Adversity, endure it.

Then difficulty will bow to you.

When working, there is no real difference
Between the important and the menial.
When serving, there is no real difference
Between the worthy and the undeserving.
When learning, there is no real difference
Between the young and the old.
When cultivating, there is no real difference
Between the sage and the ordinary.

Don't bite off more than you can chew.

Don't promise something you can't deliver.

Don't embark on a journey beyond your ability.

Don't take on more than you can handle.

Being yourself, you can take care of every moment.

Going beyond your limits, you will jeopardize your future.

Not reaching for the unattainable is the lifeline to satisfaction.

Not being opportunistic is the characteristic of contentment.

Not being conniving is the way to be honest.

Not being selfish is the way to have pure body and mind.

Don't worry that others are not treating you with respect.
Worry instead that you are not treating others with respect.

One who lacks the will to make amends is incorrigible.
One who lacks the will to do good cannot attain liberation.

Not rejecting the smallest stream,
The ocean can become an ocean.
Not cultivating small good deeds,
We cannot attain complete virtue.

If you are unwilling to reason, you are stubborn.

If you cannot reason, you are foolish.

If you are afraid to reason, you are a slave.

If you refuse to reason, you are ignorant.

Think kind thoughts,

And every day will be a good day.

Get along with your neighbors,

And every place will be a pure land.

When mixed with mud,

Even clear water becomes unclear.

When mixed with bad company,

Even an upright person becomes crooked.

It is water's nature to flow from high to low;
To overcome obstacles, the right guidance is the key.
It is human nature to look for gain;
To build good relationships, generosity is the way.

Brittle teeth break easily;
Therefore, the wise value gentleness.
Sharp blades chip easily;
Therefore, the wise value roundedness.
Dragons are rare, so seeing them is fortuitous;
Therefore, the wise value what is hidden.
The ocean is difficult to measure because it is wide;
Therefore, the wise value depth.

Use encouragement in place of criticism;
Use kindness in place of scolding;
Use caring in place of indulgence;
Use cooperation in place of detachment.

Be global in your thinking.

Be ethical in your living.

Be classical in your speech.

Be up-to-date in your learning.

When one is given, ten is returned.

When precepts are observed, action, speech, and thought are purified.

When you have patience, self and others are benefited.

When you work diligently, anything can be accomplished.

When you practice mindfulness, your body and mind are calmed.

When you have wisdom, even the smallest details are revealed.

Ridiculing others with words
Brings a deluge of problems.
Tolerating others with open-mindedness
Is a critical ingredient for blessedness.
Humiliating others with power
Invites trouble in no time.
Influencing others with ethics
Allows your reputation to live on forever.

When you consider giving as having, there is no greed.
When you consider busyness as joy, there is no bitterness.
When you consider diligence as wealth, there is no poverty.
When you consider patience as strength, there is no fear.

Through study, we learn how:

To conduct ourselves,

To reason things out,

To be aware of cause and effect,

To understand the mind.

Worldly knowledge has limits,
But the Buddha's teachings are boundless.
Worldly knowledge comes and goes,
But the Truth is always new.

Kind words without good deeds
Are equivalent to rubbish.
Good deeds without kind words
Are equivalent to nothing.

People fail because

They insist on doing things their own way.

People succeed because

They cooperate with others and do what is good.

People fail because

They have only five minutes of enthusiasm.

People succeed because

They persevere even through the last five minutes.

The best thing in the world is happiness.

The noblest deed in the world is making connections.

The greatest strength in the world is patience.

The strongest commitment in the world is willingness.

Money can buy slaves, but not good relationships.

Money can buy people, but not their hearts.

Money can buy fish and meat, but not an appetite.

Money can buy a mansion, but not peace of mind.

Money can buy beautiful clothes, but not a beautiful disposition.

Money can buy stocks and bonds, but not contentment.

Money can buy books, but not wisdom.

Money can buy a bed, but not sound sleep.

Productivity is like a money tree.

Frugality is like a treasure chest.

Diligence can gain ten thousand bushels of grain.

Mindfulness can give one the entire cosmos.

Select soldiers based on their bravery.
Hire people based on their talent.
Make decisions according to the Way.
Use money according to virtue.

Use strictness and virtue as
The principle for self-discipline.
Use kindness, honesty, loyalty, and justice as
The basis for getting along with people.
Use sincerity and diligence as
The motivation for your actions.
Use compassion and willingness as
The motivation for helping others.

Belief instilled through emotion is short-lived.
Respect earned through virtue is deep-seeded.

By being mindful of impermanence,
One can see the arising and cessation of things
And thus practice diligently.
By being mindful of no-self,
One can know one's true nature
And thus be at ease.

If your eyes can see the value of others,

You will have more help from them.

If your mouth is filled with virtuous words,

You will accumulate more merits.

If your ears are free from gossip,

You will be filled with more peace and harmony.

If your heart has the Buddha in it,

You will have more joy.

When learning, strive for depth and breadth.
When cultivating, be patient and tolerant.

The way to stay healthy is
To eat lightly, simply, and moderately.
The way to deal with life is
To bear hardships, endure losses, and be strong.

In self-observation, look within.
In self-renewal, purify continuously.
In self-practice, don't search outside.
In self-detachment, don't differentiate.

If you have farmland but never cultivate it,
You have no harvest.
If you have money but never use it,
You have no real wealth.

The mundane is illusory, but if you reject it,
Buddhahood will be difficult to achieve.
The supramundane is true, but if you are attached to it,
The light of wisdom will be obscured.

Books that speak of the truth; read as many as you can.

Books that teach right from wrong; read plenty of them.

Books that are trivial; read them sparingly.

Books that are immoral; read none at all.

In the face of death, die with a purpose–
Some deaths are weighty, like Taishan ;[1]
Other deaths are insignificant, like the feather of a goose.
In the circle of life, live with dignity–
Some lead exemplary lives
That are models for many generations to come;
Others are infamous
And their names are shunned for thousands of years.

[1] A famous mountain range in China.

As parents, we should be perfectly willing
To raise our children.
As teachers, we should be perfectly willing
To educate our students.
As students, we should be perfectly willing
To listen and learn.
As sons and daughters, we should be perfectly willing
To love and care for our parents.

When doing something new, don't be too hasty.

When dealing with people you dislike, don't be too harsh.

When persuading someone to be good, don't be too demanding.

When assigning jobs, don't be too hurried.

When listening to others, don't be inattentive.

When dealing with yourself, don't be too indulgent.

Capable people make things convenient for others everywhere.

Incapable people make things difficult for others everywhere.

If you are unwilling to learn, no one can help you.
If you are determined to learn, no one can stop you.

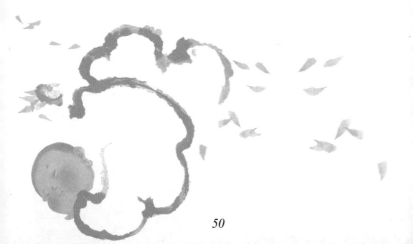

Courage grows in our minds.
Kindness blossoms in our actions.

Learning about life is more important
Than schooling.
Learning ethics is more important
Than pursuing fame and fortune.
Learning that is accessible to all is more important
Than learning reserved for the privileged.
Learning to think independently is more important
Than being spoon-fed by others.

Sit upright, like a temple bell.

Stand tall, like a pine.

Keep your bearing bright and clean, like a mirror.

Act according to principles, like the Dharma.

Think cleanly and clearly, like a river.

A writer ploughs and weeds on paper.

A farmer ploughs and weeds in the field.

A teacher ploughs and weeds on the blackboard.

A Chan practitioner ploughs and weeds in the mind.

Learning from life experience promotes good relationships.
Training the mind plants the seeds for self-improvement.

If you can overlook the faults of others,
Your practice will improve day by day.
If you expect a lot from yourself,
You will continue to learn more every day.

Without new ideas, there will be no progress.
Without a broad perspective, there will be no foresight.

While we cannot expect everything that we do to be perfect,
We should at least be responsible and strive for completion.
While we cannot expect everyone to be fully capable,
We can at least do our best and do all that we can.

Associating with the right people brings lifelong happiness.

Falling in with the wrong group of people leads to lifelong misery.

Acquiring social education enables us to make a living.

Acquiring spiritual education enables us to reach all people.

Light the mind with the lamp of wisdom.

Achieve spiritual maturity with Buddha nature.

Cure defilement with the six *paramitas*.

Enrich inner wealth with the seven *saptadhana* .[2]

---

[2] The seven sacred graces: faith, observance of precepts, listening to the Dharma, shame, remorse, renunciation, and wisdom.

Good fortune always looks with favor upon the brave.
Blessings always come to the honest and the kind.

In poverty, have loyalty and willpower.
In peril, have faith and courage.
In wealth, have kindness and generosity.
In practice, have right mind and vitality.

Knowledge helps us to manage our affairs;
If not used, it becomes useless.
The Dharma teaches us to manage our minds;
If not used, it becomes useless.

The Dharma has no good or bad;

The distinction arises from perception.

Conditions are neither favorable nor unfavorable;

The distinction is only present in the minds of people.

One who never tires of learning is wise.

One who never tires of teaching is benevolent.

One who enjoys work is diligent.

One who never complains about hardships is capable.

Self-understanding and discipline are the keys
To conducting oneself in society.
Tolerating and helping others is the nourishment
For establishing good relationships.

Understanding suffering,

You will be content and not demanding.

Understanding remorse,

You will progress and not regress.

By having the courage to ask questions, wisdom will grow.

By being able to listen, learning will take place.

By being skillful in communication, understanding will develop.

By thinking without boundaries, creativity will result.

By being willing to face challenges, strength will increase.

By practicing meditation, virtues will grow.

Trusting what others say without observing what they do
Is the folly of the wise.
Trusting what others do without observing what they say
Is the wisdom of the foolish.
Observing what others say and what they do
Is the wisdom of the wise.
Neither observing what others say nor what they do
Is the folly of the foolish.

Self-learning is the impetus for success.

Self-discipline is the prerequisite for success.

Self-confidence is the road map to success.

Self-respect is the key to success.

Self-planning leads to happiness.

Self-improvement increases knowledge.

Self-control enhances well-being.

Self-application leads to success.

Truth relies on determination to actualize it.
Determination relies on truth to realize it.

To develop oneself, one must endure any challenge.

To resolve conflicts, one must bear any responsibility.

To experience life,
One must rely on ethics to form moral integrity.
To pursue knowledge,
One must rely on wisdom to broaden the mind.

In learning—listen, think, and cultivate;

Then speak, write, and act.

Maintain the precepts, concentration, and wisdom;

Then your life will be peaceful and happy.

To have good health, eat moderately.

To have good relationships, be sincere and humble.

To have a good family, be caring.

To have a good career, be diligent.

Taking refuge in the Triple Gem is the spirit of equality
Because the Buddha and sentient beings are all the same,
Without differentiation.
Observing the Five Precepts is the respect for freedom
Because, by not offending others,
We all benefit.

When we can see through delusions,
Vitality and opportunity abound.
When we cannot see through delusions,
Obstacles and hardships abound.

Research needs data and information.

Creativity calls for talent.

Study requires deep thinking.

Action demands judging right from wrong.

Be an upright person
Who behaves righteously and virtuously.
Don't be a wicked person
Who behaves with no sense of right or wrong.

A person's character

Can influence his whole life.

A community's character

Can impact the whole nation for many generations to come.

Time is given second by second;
You should use it second by second.
Books are written word by word;
You should read them word by word.

With an open mind, every road is wide.

With a pure mind, everywhere is the pure land.

Being able to suffer losses, one may gain an advantage.
Being able to bear hardships, one may gain happiness.
Being able to be friendly, one may gain strength.
Being able to give, one may gain good fortune.

Dealing with people should be like rolling a snowball;
The more you roll it, the more relationships you have.
Performing tasks should be like weaving a tapestry;
The more you weave, the more accomplishments you have.

By not rejecting small streams, oceans form.
By not denying the earth, mountains grow.
By not being ashamed to ask, knowledge increases.
By not covering up mistakes, perfection arises.

In dealing with people–
Be comfortable with circumstances,
Accept conditions as they arise,
Follow your heart with ease,
Feel happy when others do good.
In dealing with things–
Start with the basics,
Pay attention where there are doubts,
Take action where there is nothing,
Work hard where there is weakness.

To accomplish large tasks, be determined.

To accomplish small tasks, be attentive.

To accomplish difficult tasks, be patient.

To accomplish good deeds, expect no reward.

In performing tasks, know your limits.
It is not easy to succeed if you ignore the parts
While grasping for the whole.
In dealing with people, know their abilities.
It is easy to fail if you ignore their strengths
While focusing on their weaknesses.

By nourishing and cherishing talent,
You can hand down the light.
Through teaching and working with people,
You can pass down a legacy.

By cultivating the motivation to teach oneself,
One will not regress in times of leisure.
By cultivating the compassion to teach others,
One can pass on one's experiences.

Cultivate interests,
But don't become obsessed.
Learn to be morally upright,
But don't become ultraconservative.

Only through action can we accomplish a goal.

Only through contemplation and practice can we reach nirvana.

Searching for truth is the highest human hope.
Propagating truth is the ultimate human mission.

The program of education is to stimulate the mind.

The key to education is to instruct according to potential.

The foundation of education resides in the habits of daily life.

The purpose of education is to develop character.

If the reasoning is unclear,

It's difficult to accomplish things.

If things don't transpire,

It's difficult to demonstrate the reasoning.

Learning is to know how to question
Even after you have learned.
Traveling and studying is to learn more
Even after you have traveled.

Although carelessness may easily result in mistakes,
Over-carefulness can easily spoil things as well.

By being mindful everywhere, one observes problems.
By investigating everything, one resolves problems.

The best approach to negotiation
Is to start with what is beneficial to the other party.
The greatest affinity created
Is to help others succeed.

To outside temptation you must be
As unenticed as still water and dead ashes.
To the pursuit of knowledge you must be
As vigorous as a wildfire.

The way to longevity is through
Virtue, achievements, and inspirational writings.
The way to prosperity is through
Credibility, responsibility, and diligence.

Give confidence to others,

Give joy to others,

Give hope to others,

Make things convenient for others–

Giving has limitless, ingenious uses.

Understand tolerance,

Understand peace,

Understand modesty,

Understand respect–

Understanding provides limitless, ingenious solutions.

Know how to listen–you will accept the Dharma.

Know how to think–you will benefit from the Dharma.

Know how to cultivate–you will apply the Dharma.

The wise nourish the mind.
The foolish nourish the body.
The ethical nourish virtues.
The wicked nourish power.

No money, no opportunity–

Let it be,

Cultivate merit and wisdom to reach nirvana.

Little clothing, little food–

Let it be,

Seek treasure in your mind.

When stating opinions,

Don't be afraid of being general and uncritical,

But rather of being childish and meaningless.

When beginning to write,

Don't worry about having no material,

But rather about having no words and substance.

Making good use of fragments of time
Is a good recipe for making progress.
Treasuring every opportunity
Is the wonder drug for conducting worldly affairs.

Don't overuse your authority, or you will collapse
Don't overuse your fortune and merits, or you will decay.

Feeling moved is momentary,
To be genuinely moved lasts a lifetime.
Gaining benefit is momentary,
To gain genuine benefit lasts a lifetime.

The most artistic way to communicate is
With complete heart-to-heart understanding,
Without words.
The highest state of doing things is
With everything in complete understanding,
Without forms.

Knowing how to read books

Is not as good as knowing how to read people.

Knowing how to read people

Is not as good as knowing how to understand people.

Knowing how to understand people

Is not as good as knowing how to utilize people's strengths.

Knowing how to utilize people's strengths

Is not as good as knowing how to get along with people.

All phenomena are conditional;
Don't try to force events.
Only if causes and conditions exist,
Can everything be fulfilled.

Experience can teach people astuteness;
Suffering losses can teach people caution.

Where justice is, don't fall behind.
Where profit is, don't jump ahead.

If you are not completely honest,
Then your mind cannot concentrate.
If your faith is not completely focused,
Then your words cannot be carried out.

Experience joy through modesty.

Cultivate virtue through tolerance.

Overcome desire through self-control.

Calm body and mind through tranquility.

Gathering and educating the world's gifted
Is a pleasure in life.
Being close to a master and learning from him
Is a blessing in life.

Virtues—don't reject them for being old.
Knowledge—don't reject it for being new.

Dreams open the door to idealism.
Idealism paves the way to success.

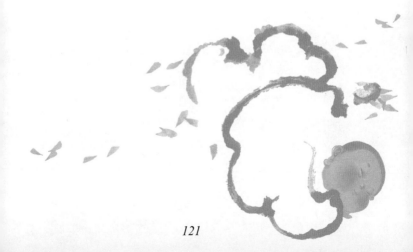

The joy from contentment is limitless.
The suffering from greed is endless.

Those who are doubtful are doubted.
Those who are neglectful are neglected.

Dust is not small;
The cosmos is not huge.
One is not trivial;
A billion is not plenty.

Happiness is nothing more than being free from worry.

Suffering is nothing more then having excessive desires.

Wealth is nothing more than being content.

Poverty is nothing more than being greedy.

Those who constantly strengthen their virtues
By reforming their ways are called virtuous people.
Those who spread their vices
By covering their mistakes are called common people.

Those who treasure wisdom manage not only profit,
But also culture.
Those who pursue kindness manage not only themselves,
But also morality and justice.
Those who cherish etiquette manage not only wealth,
But also good company.
Those who admire the Way manage not only happiness,
But also Dharma joy.

Learning, and being able to apply it, is real learning.

Knowing, and being able to implement it, is real knowing.

Real learning and real knowing are wisdom.

In learning Chan, first learn to be modest,
Then the Chan mind will exist.
In cultivating purity, first cultivate respect,
Then the pure land will exist.

Learning Buddhism is to learn mainly about yourself;
So you must search for, and inquire into, the original mind.
Learning Chan is to apply your own mind;
So you must investigate and study the original face.

Knowledge makes people humble.

Ignorance makes people arrogant.

Modesty makes people noble.

Conceit makes people shallow.

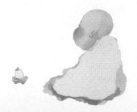

Knowledge is acquired through experiences,
Talent is shown in circumstances.

When learning, emulate the sages.

When comparing, use the sages as the standard.

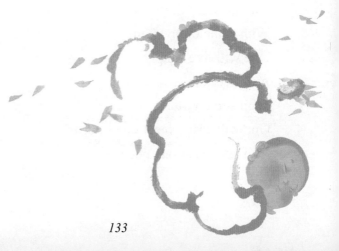

With some exposure to Buddhism,
One will make earnest efforts to cultivate virtue
And achieve morality.
With some grasp of the universe,
One will make further progress
And greater improvement.
With some cultivation,
One will live simply
And live freely.
With some virtue,
One will easily meet one's needs
And take what one needs.

Although being a leader is good
Because you can lead the community,
Being second is also wonderful
Because you can complement and support others.
A leader should take care of the weak;
Secondaries should respect the elder.

Trees won't grow tall
Without enduring the sun and the rain.
Character won't be developed completely
Without being tempered by hardships and suffering.

By comprehending no-self
You realize letting go of the self,
Merging into the spiritual self
And having more.
By experiencing no-self
You can understand giving charity and joyful giving,
Sharing with all beings
And having the self everywhere.

Get along in harmony with all people;
Make good use of money;
Be sparing with clothing and food;
Make body and mind pure and dignified;
Be one with nature, in mutual respect.

The wise, who understand eternity,
Know how to utilize time.
The sage, who understands boundlessness,
Knows how to utilize space.

Medicine is not good or bad;
When it cures, it is good.
Dharma is not superior or inferior;
When it is applicable, it is superior.

The purpose of study is to have understanding.
The purpose of education is to be a good person.

Reform comes from determination.

Innovation comes from concentration.

Education comes from compassion.

Service comes from willingness.

The right way to study is nothing more
Than reading more and memorizing more.
The path to writing is nothing more
Than thinking more and writing more.

Studying can improve one;

Teaching can improve one even more.

Paying respect to the Buddha can give one confidence;

Practicing Buddhism can give one even more confidence.

To show rightness, one must first destroy vices;
To spread purity, one must first eliminate impurity.

By observing a tree's shadow,
You know its height.
By observing a person's intentions,
You know his virtues.

Purifying the mind is the fundamental goal of education.

Changing one's temperament is the greatest benefit of studying.

Have real recognition of the concept of time and space.

Have historical knowledge of the concept of tradition.

Have universal recognition of the concept of culture.

Have truthful recognition of the concept of belief.

Being diligent,

You naturally have more time than others.

Being active,

You naturally have more space than others.

Being able to endure hardships,

You naturally have more success than others.

The idea of the Buddha
Exceeds divine power;
You are in charge of your own destiny.
The idea of the pure land
Can achieve the ideal of the right to live;
Foster the state of equality.

If you apply the Buddha's teachings,
You can resolve things.
If you rely on the Buddha's teachings,
You can live with ease.

Uphold the precepts, or you
Will cut off the road to the human and heavenly realms.
Cultivate virtue, or meritorious work
Will be incomplete.
Study sutras, or logical thought
Will be unclear.
Practice meditation, or your mind
Will be impure.
Understand the Way, or you
Will encounter obstacles.

A word of truth is priceless,

A thousand times more precious than gold or silver.

Human virtue is priceless,

A thousand times higher than the highest mountain.

A tolerant mind can embrace "great" and "more."

A responsible courage can bear honor and shame.

A decisive wisdom can determine right and wrong.

A kind-hearted moment will bring endless merit.

A pure-hearted moment will bring innumerable virtue.

An enlightened moment will bring infinite wonder.

A moment of *sunyata*[3] will bring the essence of formlessness.

[3] Emptiness

One useful word is worth more
Than innumerable, useless words;
One beneficial act is better
Than many useless hardships.

One kind word is like
The fragrance of flowers in paradise.
One harsh word is like
A sword in hell.

Comfort and happiness are the baits
That poison determination;
Suffering is the foundry
That forms sages.

A quick learner is not necessarily smart.
A slow learner is not necessarily stupid.

Being unconventional

Does not necessarily mean being outstanding.

Being mild-mannered

Does not necessarily mean being unintelligent.

Learning should be like a pyramid,
Wide and tall.
In conducting oneself, one should behave like a sage,
With merit, wisdom, and character.

A little sincerity, and all conditions will respond.
A lot of gratitude, and the world will be joyful.

To urge others to be good,

You must first be upright yourself;

That is, "Do as I do" is better than "Do as I say."

To defend oneself against rumors,

You must first be upstanding;

That is, "facts speak louder than words."

Aspiring to the right Path,
One must first have the right mind.
Entering into the right Path,
One must be able to let go.
Practicing the right Path,
One must use compassionate wisdom.
Realizing the right Path,
One must comprehend no-self.

Where the Dharma exists, the Buddha exists;
Believing in the Dharma is believing in the Buddha.
Where the sangha resides, the Dharma resides;
Believing in the sangha is believing in the Dharma.

Without cultivation, you cannot liberate yourself.

Without teaching the Dharma, you cannot liberate all beings.

Attribute glory to the Buddha;

Attribute accomplishments to all beings;

Attribute benefits to the monastics;

Attribute merits to devotees.

Fame and wealth are transitory;

Only achievement and character are truly beneficial.

The world is like a house on fire;

Only calming the body and mind is the true pure land.

Understanding classical lessons can alert the mind.
Limiting alcohol and sex can purify the mind.
Eliminating personal desire can cultivate the mind.
Realizing the truth can clear the mind.

The breeze feels cool and lovely;
Kind words feel gentle and loving.

People who are rich in heart–for the favor of one drop of water,
They will return a fountain.
People who are poor in heart–to give one thing away
Is as difficult as climbing to the sky.

Before learning, one should focus
On pursuing what one wants to learn.
After learning, one should focus
On applying what one has already learned.

Language should be fluent,
But more importantly, be proper.
Clothes should be simple,
But more importantly, be suitable.

Essays should be smooth,
But more importantly, meaningful.
Expressions should precise,
But more importantly, sincere.

Making earnest efforts to cultivate virtue
Is the direct route to getting along with people.
Forming affinities
Is the resource for performing tasks.

Better to uphold the precepts imperfectly
Than to misunderstand the Dharma, thereby losing faith.

Using useless words to occupy useful time
Not only makes people disgusted but also virtueless.
Using useful time to do useless things
Is not only unhelpful but also a waste of life.

Don't rush, don't rush, safety first.
Don't rush, don't rush, modesty first.
Don't rush, don't rush, courtesy first.

Indulgence is the root of all evil.

Diligence is the key to good deeds.

Use some thought to treat evil thought;

Use correct thought to treat delusive thought;

Use absence of delusive thought to treat correct thought.

Don't use a little knowledge to acquire a lot of honor;
Use all of your ability to bear most of the duty;
Use full preparation to teach a complete course;
Use all your heart to return even a small favor.

Accomplishing the Way depends on oneself;

Applying the Way depends on time;

Perfecting the Way depends on people;

Realizing the Way depends on cultivation.

ABOUT THE TRANSLATORS

Tom Manzo received his Ph.D. from Yale University in Golden Age Spanish Literature, and is currently a Professor of Spanish and Latin at San Antonio College, Texas. He took his Bodhisattva Precepts in 1997.

Shujan Cheng is a life-long Buddhist. Originally from Taiwan, she completed her studies in the United States in Economics and Finance. She taught Economics and Finance for fifteen years before deciding to dedicate herself to translating Buddhist texts.